LEADERS OF
ANCIENT ROME

NERO

Destroyer of Rome

CONTENTS

ITALY AT THE TIME OF NERO

Luca

ETRURIA

ITALIA

Roma

Tusculum

Arpinum

Astura

Formiae

Puteoli

Via Appia

SARDINIA

MEDITERRANEAN SEA

Lilybaeum

SICILIA

Syracusae

Born to rule

CHAPTER 1

2
3
4
5
6
7

When future emperor Nero was born on December 15, AD 37, his father, Cnaeus Domitius Aheno-barbus, said that any child of his would have a detestable nature and would become a public danger. This prophetic remark was not a good start for the boy, whose full name at birth was Lucius Domitius Ahenobarbus. His family had a reputation for cruelty, arrogance, and extravagance, which had passed down through the generations to this child.

Nero's grandfather had been famous for his skill as a charioteer and had been decorated after a military campaign in Germany, though he was also known as a vicious individual. Nero's father was said to have killed a freedman of his for refusing to drink as much as he was told to, to have gouged out the eye of a nobleman in the Forum, and to

A statue of Nero as a young man

have deliberately run over and killed a boy on the Appian Way.

By the time Nero was three, his father was dead and his mother, Agrippina, had been banished by the emperor Caligula for being involved in a conspiracy against him. So Nero's early childhood was spent with his aunt. His mother was allowed back into Rome after Caligula's death, when

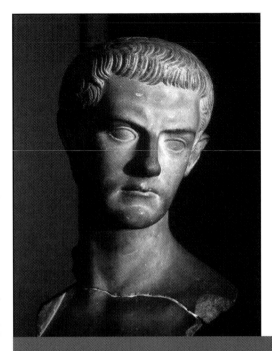

Gaius Julius Caesar Germanicus, known as Caligula, emperor of Rome from AD 37 to 41

Claudius became emperor in AD 41, and she eventually became the new emperor's fourth wife. It was Agrippina's evil character that shaped Nero and determined many of the events of history to follow, including his rise to power.

Agrippina was notoriously lax in her morals, using her beauty as a weapon to secure wealth and fame. She managed and manipulated her new husband Claudius so that Britannicus, his son from a former marriage, was sidelined in favor of his new stepson, Nero. Agrippina also

A stone bust of Claudius, who became emperor upon the death of Caligula in AD 41 and ruled until AD 54

arranged the murder of Domitia Lepida, the aunt who had looked after Nero during her time away from Rome in exile. This may have been because Domitia was Britannicus's grandmother, and would be likely to support his cause.

Nero was made consul designate at a very early age, soon after putting on his toga of manhood in AD 51. This meant that the highest political office in Rome had been reserved for him, though he would not hold the post for another four years. In the meantime he was called the prince of the youth. Rather ironically, he was also designated the protector of Britannicus, on the suggestion of the emperor's freedman Pallas. A marriage to Claudius's daughter Octavia was arranged for him by his mother in AD 53 to strengthen Nero's closeness to the emperor. This came about even though Octavia had already been betrothed to another man, the hapless Lucius Junius Silanus Torquatus, who was accused of incest with his sister and thrown out of the Senate, according to the historian Tacitus.

However, Agrippina worried more and more that her own boy, Nero, might be hampered in his path to power by his stepbrother Britannicus as he grew older, so she met with the known poisoner Locusta. She arranged to murder her husband Claudius by giving him poisoned mushrooms to eat, before he could take steps to help move his own son's career forward. In the wake of Claudius's death, on October 13, AD 54, Nero was proclaimed emperor by the praetorian guards, the handpicked bodyguard of the imperial family, who took him to the Senate where the fathers of the city accepted him. Nero was sixteen years old and had just become ruler of the mightiest empire in the world.

Agrippina, Nero's mother, who poisoned her husband Claudius

From the age of ten, Nero had been taught by one of the leading literary figures of his day, Lucius Annaeus Seneca, who now stayed with the young emperor as his advisor. Seneca had originally come from Cordoba in Spain and was a remarkably wealthy and powerful man. He was well known as an orator, writer, and a Stoic philosopher, though he had been exiled some years before to Corsica for having an adulterous affair with Claudius's niece, Julia Livilla. It was thanks to the influence of Agrippina that he had been restored to Rome, some time after she married Claudius. Seneca was assisted by Sextus Afranius Burrus, the prefect of the guard who had engineered Nero's proclamation as emperor, and by Nero's mother, who stayed as close as she could to the center of power. While Seneca provided the intelligence and academic stimulus, Burrus was a calm and controlled individual who originally came from Vaison la Romaine in the south of France and had a very real strength of character. Both men were extremely wealthy, having financial interests and influence spreading far across the Roman Empire.

For some time, it appeared that the young emperor and his trio of helpers would rule Rome well, and he seemed to heed the advice he was given. People overlooked the rumors of

Claudius's murder, and when Nero spoke about him publicly he did so with respect.

Objects belonging to a Roman schoolboy

Claudius was made a god, and a temple to him was built on the Caelian Hill in Rome.

A GOOD BEGINNING

It was important that Nero's image be kept as clean as possible at the outset of his reign, and Seneca urged him to make "clemency" his watchword. Clemency meant that Nero would be understanding and forgiving, an emperor of the people who would try his best to emulate Augustus, the first emperor of Rome. Whereas

Claudius had been very obviously influenced, and to some extent controlled, by his personal staff of freedmen, Nero said that he would listen to advisers and restore some power to the Senate. He wanted to put an end to trials carried out in the emperor's personal rooms, separating the imperial house from the process of law and government more than had been the case under his predecessor. He tried to appear forgiving and to create an image for himself of kindness. He once said, "How I wish I had never learned to write!" when asked to sign an execution order. The Senate placed restrictions on lawyers, preventing them from taking fees or bribes. At the same time, Nero relaxed the need for junior magistrates to put on gladiatorial shows, which was expensive and therefore restricted some men from being able to hold official posts. Also, Nero rejected the Senate's offers to call him "Father of the Country" and to change the beginning of the year to December, when he had been born.

Furthermore, Nero made it unnecessary for consuls to swear an oath to support the emperor rather than the state, making it seem that he had a genuinely positive attitude to shared government. He allowed Plautius Lateranus to return to Rome from exile. Lateranus had been thrown out by Claudius for having an affair with his third wife, Messallina. It seemed that Nero would be a considerate and careful emperor by listening to the advice of the Senate, acknowledging its advice, and even refusing its offer of a perpetual consulship. Coins from the time bear an acknowledgment of the Senate's approval of their issue, which is a tangible sign of his respect. This was a good start, though a good number of problems would have to be solved soon.

Agrippina became Nero's co-ruler, which was not mandated by law but was recognized in a variety of other ways. Nero is said to have used the password "the best of mothers" with his palace guards, and early coins of the reign show both Nero's and Agrippina's heads facing each other. Although she was not allowed to attend Senate meetings, a door was built to the rear of the Senate house so she could listen in on the debates. On one occasion, Nero was sitting on a platform waiting to receive a delegation of Armenians. As they approached, his mother seemed to try to move next to him. Seneca told the young man to stand and advance to meet the embassy, thus avoiding a breach of protocol. At that time a woman would not have been allowed to stand on the imperial dais next to the emperor in this way without compromising his authority.

Messalina, holding her infant son Britannicus, whom Nero would later poison to secure the throne for himself

It seems, however, that mother and son often did not see eye to eye, and quarrels soon arose between them. Her affair with the freedman Pallas, who had been a senior executive and financial secretary on Claudius's staff, led to real disagreement, resulting in the dismissal of Pallas from the imperial household in AD 55. At this time Agrippina thought she was losing influence with her son and considered promoting the interests of her stepson Britannicus, who in many ways would have been a natural heir to the throne of his father Claudius, with a better claim to power than Nero had.

As Britannicus neared the age of fourteen and was about to put on his man's toga for the first time, Nero keenly felt the threat of his presence. This fear resulted in Britannicus's death, poisoned at the dinner table by his step-brother, Nero, who then claimed Britannicus must have had an epileptic fit. This heartless and callous murder of an innocent boy is perhaps the first time that Nero's true character emerged. The son was beginning to show the same tendencies as his mother, mimicking when she had murdered her husband Claudius in order to remove him from the throne.

FIVE GOOD YEARS

CHAPTER 2

1
3
4
5
6
7

The emperor Trajan once described the first five years of Nero's rule as one of the best times in Rome's history, though in some ways this is hard to understand. Certainly it was a time of great palace intrigue, with Burrus, Seneca, and Agrippina all seeking to influence the young emperor in their various ways. Agrippina felt unhappy about several of Nero's love affairs, including one with the freedwoman Acte.

In these early years Nero seems to have kept some very unhealthy company, parading through the streets of Rome late at night, causing mayhem and havoc wherever he went. The historian Tacitus says that Rome came to resemble a conquered city at times. Sometimes the riotous behavior caused real problems, as when Senator Julius Montanus was involved in a brawl with Nero. Later on, the senator sent a letter apologizing to the emperor for hitting him, but he was then forced to commit suicide for this action.

AGRIPPINA OUT OF FAVOR

One of the emperor's good friends, Marcus Salvius Otho (who later became emperor himself for a short time), had a very

A bust of Nero, Rome's fifth emperor

attractive wife named Poppaea who was keen to advance herself by any means possible. Otho was eventually sent away to be governor of the Spanish province of Lusitania so that Nero and Poppaea could carry on an affair in his absence. This caused great annoyance to Agrippina, who urged Nero to stick with his wife Octavia, but he had little love for Claudius's daughter and the rift between mother and son grew.

Gradually Agrippina lost her influence with Nero, and her image no longer appeared

The villa of Poppaea at Oplontis. Poppaea was Nero's favorite after he had Agrippina killed.

opposite his on coins. Agrippina's imperial guards were taken away from her, and she was removed from Nero's palace in Rome. It was reported that she wanted to marry Rubellius Plautus, the grandson of the emperor Tiberius, and that she would then try to rule without Nero. In the meantime there were more rumors. One was that Seneca and Burrus were plotting to replace Nero with Claudius's grandson, Faustus Cornelius Sulla Felix, who was eventually sent off in exile to Massilia, modern-day Marseilles, in France.

However, Nero seems to have been advised well for much of this time; his personal popularity in Rome was considerable. How far he formulated his own policy and how far he was ruled by the philosopher and the guard prefect we cannot ascertain, but many measures taken at the time kept his people happy. In particular, Nero attempted to keep the grain supply secure, completing improvements to the harbor in Ostia. He also ensured that grain ships were not counted as taxable property, thus making them a good business investment. Twice, a donation of 400 sesterces was made to each citizen of Rome. On another occasion 40 million sesterces were paid into the public treasury to maintain public credit levels. Nero attempted to reduce the number of taxes levied on goods traded, though in this he was not entirely successful. He did abolish a 4 percent tax on slaves. Tax claims going back more than one year were abandoned and soldiers were exempted from paying any tax at all except on what they sold.

Nero helped many retired soldiers settle into homes and improved the political status of some towns as part of this drive. Pompeii and Tegeanum became Roman coloniae, which meant that their citizens had full Roman citizenship, which at that time was not normal throughout the Italian peninsula. In AD 57 Nero built a new amphitheater for public entertainments in the Campus Martius area of Rome, declaring, however, that nobody should be allowed to die there for the sake of entertainment. He also declared that senators should fight in the arena, which was not at all a popular suggestion with them. Nero held the office of consul in AD 55, 57, 58, and 60. He showed his respect for the Senate on a good many occasions. Once, after a riot in the amphitheater in Pompeii in AD 59, he referred the case for judgment to the Senate, which then banned the Pompeians from holding any more gladiatorial games for ten years.

A wall painting of a bird eating nuts, from Poppaea's villa

Five years after becoming emperor, in AD 59, Nero had become so resentful of his mother that he resolved to have her killed. There are different stories about their relationship, and they may even have been lovers. But it seems that it was particularly due to Agrippina's dislike of Poppaea that Nero made his decision. He may also have been influenced by his lover's resentment, as Poppaea made fun of him, calling him a mother's boy. He called his advisers together and consulted with them about how to murder Agrippina, relying heavily on his ex-tutor, a freedman called Anicetus. The decision was made to invite Agrippina to dinner at Baiae near Naples, on the coast of Italy, and then take her home in a ship that would be so constructed as to collapse and sink during the voyage. When the lead-weighted canopy over her head fell down, however, Agrippina was saved by the arms of her couch, which stuck out and prevented her

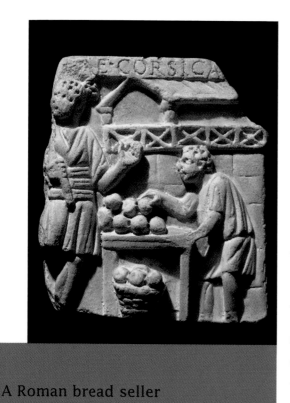

A Roman bread seller

from being crushed by the debris. Her maid Acerronia called out for help, saying that she was Agrippina and in need of help, but she was killed by a blow to the head from an oar. This was a warning to her mistress that it was a real murder attempt, not an accident. She then swam to shore and managed to return to her villa in safety, though in some considerable distress now about what might happen to her next.

Nero then received a message from Agerinus, a freedman of Agrippina, who came to him to announce her "fortunate" survival. A knife was planted on the unlucky Agerinus, who was accused of coming to murder the emperor on his mistress's orders. Nero then sent Anicetus to Agrippina's house at night to murder her. She had been deserted by all her slaves and was found by her assassins when

Roman ivory hatpins

they burst into her chamber. She urged her killer to strike her in her womb, where Nero had been born. It is said that the emperor went to see the corpse of his mother and admired her physical beauty as she lay dead before him. Nero now became terrified of public outcry and spread the rumor that Agrippina had tried to kill him, and declared her birthday a day of ill-omen. He wrote to the Senate, saying she had been killed after Agerinus's attempt on his life. She had interfered in government and her death was an act of providence.

After the murder of Agrippina, Nero's so-called five good years came to an end. It seems that while his mother was alive she may have caused him to use restraint which, when combined with the influence of Seneca and Burrus, had held him in check. His popularity with the upper classes of Rome began to suffer, as they regarded his actions as insulting and demeaning to them. The evil side of his nature began to be more apparent as he began to act more like an autocratic monarch than an emperor who upheld the ancient republican traditions. When a bolt of lightning struck his villa in Subiaco in AD 60, rumors arose that this meant the occupant of the throne would soon be replaced. So Nero took the opportunity of banishing to Asia Rubellius Plautus, a descendant of Tiberius and therefore someone who could have had a claim to the throne.

GAMES AND PLAYS

From AD 59, Nero began to collect around himself a group of young men enlisted from the upper classes, whom he called the Augustans. They were a sort of private bodyguard or entourage. These young men would join him in gymnastic or artistic performances, lending support to his wish to perform in public.

Nero was a very keen showman who had a passion to take part in all kinds of activities. He had a private circus, or racetrack, built for him in the Vatican valley where he competed as a singer and charioteer before his selected public. It is hard to understand today how much impact this would have had then. The performing arts were seen as degrading, something to be done by Greeks for Roman entertainment. In wanting to sing, recite, and compete, Nero was behaving in a rather un-Roman way.

The theater at Nico-polis. Nero probably performed here.

The members of the Senate and other nobles who were compelled to witness such activities must have felt very uncomfortable. It is interesting to note that ordinary Roman citizens, or plebeians, probably enjoyed the shows and the chance to see their emperor perform in person, but this was never reflected in the reaction of the upper classes.

Nero, however, was undeterred. It seems that his enthusiasm knew no restraint, and he hurled himself into his performances with increasing determination. He raced chariots around his circus and celebrated his *lud juvenales*, or young men's games, where he shaved off his beard in public. He had voice training and even embarked on strange diets to improve the quality of his singing, lying down with sheets of lead on his chest to improve his diaphragm. Historians believe that he refrained from eating apples, as they may have been bad for his voice.

In AD 60 Nero instituted the first so-called Neronia, or Nero's Games, where he staged events including athletics, chariot racing, musical contests, poetry recitals, and even oratories. The games were to be held every fifth year and were held again in AD 65, but were discontinued

thereafter. This was an attempt to have an event in Rome along

the lines of the Olympic Games. Nero himself competed as a harpist and also won a prize for oratory. Many of the Augustans also competed, as did others, including professional athletes.

In AD 61, Nero built a gymnasium in Rome and encouraged senators and other nobles to attend. He even offered them free oil with which to anoint themselves. Nero also built a complex of baths in the city. He carried on with his literary efforts, completing a poem called the *Sack of Troy*, which was to get him into trouble in later times. It has been suggested

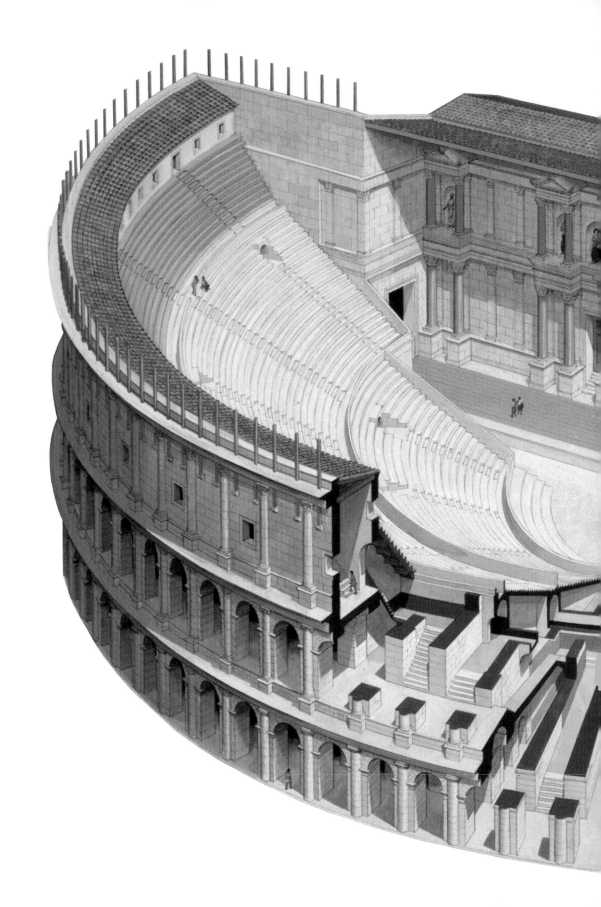

that Nero may have had some real ability as a writer, perhaps more so than as a singer, since despite all his training and dieting he apparently had a thin and rather reedy voice.

Nero's suspicion of the upper-class Romans around him grew as their hostility to his hobbies made them withdraw from him.

The death of the guard prefect Burrus in AD 62 may have been due to natural causes, though there were some suggestions that Nero had him poisoned for some unknown reason. Seneca asked to retire, but Nero would not allow him to do so, saying he still needed his advice and help. The emperor appointed two successors to the post of guard prefect, Faenius Rufus and Gaius Ofonius Tigellinus, the latter a low-born Sicilian who had previously suffered banishment from Italy for his crimes. Tigellinus had a marked effect on Nero and seems to have been a terrible influence on him.

An artist's depiction of the Theater of Marcellus

One of Tigellinus's early achievements was to persuade Nero to have Rubellius

35

Roman mosaics showing theater masks worn by actors during their performances

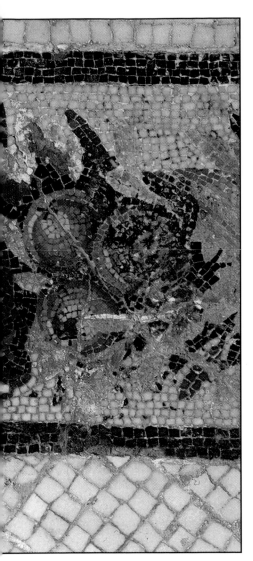

Plautus killed in Asia where he was in exile, along with Faustus Cornelius Sulla Felix, who was in exile in Massilia. Plautus's head was brought to Nero, who is said to have exclaimed aloud to himself, "Nero, how could you have been so frightened of such a long-nosed man?" Sulla's head was brought to him, too, which Nero mocked for its gray hair.

The Senate reacted to this by congratulating Nero on his escape from the treachery of Plautus and Sulla, which may have only served to feed the emperor's growing self-deception. It seemed that Nero could do no wrong, but if he did, the Senate would not only forgive him but even give praise. Two nobles, Antistius Sosianus and Fabricius Veiento, were tried for treason and banished, which seems relatively lucky for them, when compared with the fate of so many others. Sosianus had been accused of reciting improper

The theater at Delphi. Delphi was symbolic of the best of Greek culture for the Romans. Nero probably performed here.

satirical verses about the emperor at a dinner party. Nero had wanted a worse punishment than banishment for him, but the Senate's decision was a lenient one. Veiento was found guilty of using improper influence with Nero and of insulting senators and priests.

A ROMAN DIVORCE

As a sign of his growing independence, Nero decided in AD 62 that his marriage to Octavia should be brought to an end. In a shameful deal that he struck with his freedman Anicetus, Octavia was accused of committing adultery with Anicetus and banished to the island of Pandateria, where she was later killed, her veins cut open as she lay in a hot bath. Her head was brought to Nero's mistress, Poppaea, the historian Tacitus tells us. Anicetus himself was allowed to retire to the island of Sardinia as a reward for his lies, while Nero was free to marry Poppaea. Later in the same year she gave birth to a daughter, Claudia, who died about four months later. Poppaea took the name Augusta.

During the following year, AD 63, Nero performed in the theater at Neapolis, modern-day Naples, which marked a turn in his confidence.

Before this, he had only appeared with self-selected groups and in private venues, but now he was becoming more open in his desire to stand before the public. Tacitus tells us that Nero chose Naples because it was (in origin at least) a Greek city where his art would be appreciated. Nero had plans to go to Greece and Egypt, but these were cancelled at the last minute. He toured Greece four years later in a great spectacle of entertainment, but in the meantime he returned to Rome.

ABUSE OF POWER

Nero had an ongoing fear of those whose claim to the throne might challenge his, and this was reflected in his uncertainty as to how far he could go as absolute ruler without causing a crisis of government. An example of this occurred in AD 63. The great-great-grandson of Augustus, Decimus Junius Silanus Torquatus, was required to commit suicide after informers accused him of plotting against the emperor. Nero's personal conduct progressed from bad to worse—he held a fake wedding, a so-called marriage to a young man called Pythagoras. It was in AD 64, however, that things got particularly out of hand, and the scale of Nero's excessive ambition was seen for the first time by everyone around him.

THE FIRE

On July 18, AD 64, fire broke out in Rome, starting in the Circus Maximus and spreading eventually to ten of the fourteen districts of the city. The devastation of Rome was on a scale never previously known and for nine days the fire raged wildly. Some of Rome's most historic buildings were destroyed forever, including the famous Temple of Jupiter built by Romulus and the Temple of Vesta.

Nero—who at the time was staying in Antium, where he was born—returned to Rome, and apparently took the lead in fire-fighting activities. Nonetheless, stories got out that instead he had been involved in a dramatic production, performing his poem about the sack of Troy in the Tower of Maecenas, overlooking the destruction. The story says that Nero "fiddled while Rome burned," referring to his ability as a kithara player (a kithara was a stringed instrument, a sort of early guitar or violin). But should we believe this account? Probably not, though we cannot know for sure. He certainly did take steps to alleviate the suffering of his people by opening public buildings and his own gardens to the homeless. He also lowered

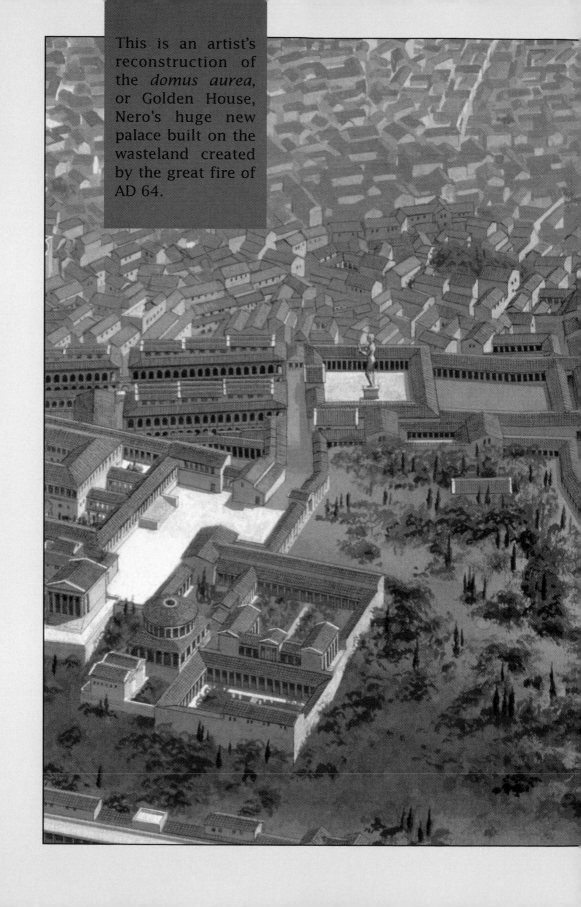

This is an artist's reconstruction of the *domus aurea*, or Golden House, Nero's huge new palace built on the wasteland created by the great fire of AD 64.

the price of grain and helped to secure extra deliveries to the city from the port of Ostia.

However, it was during the aftermath of the fire that Nero laid himself open to personal attacks. He set about rebuilding the city with a positive attitude, laying down special regulations about new buildings so that each would have a colonnade at the front. Height restrictions were imposed as well. Builders were rewarded for keeping to their contracts or finishing their projects early, and many of the new constructions had to be carried out in stone, not wood. Nero even saw to it that the grain ships took the debris out of Rome when returning to Ostia. This was all seen as positive, but Nero earned much criticism when he undertook the biggest and most expensive building project ever seen in Rome, that of his famous Golden House.

The Golden House, or *domus aurea*, was a huge new palace, built to replace the previous, so-called *domus transitoria*, or corridor palace, which had connected the Palatine and Caelian Hills. The plan was to build not just between these hills, but also to extend the complex across onto the Esquiline Hill. The Golden House surpassed the earlier construction to an unbelievable degree. By using the wasteland created by the fire, Nero created a huge park with lakes, lawns, and woodlands. The great house was faced with gold leaf and surrounded by a colonnade up to a mile in length, if we can believe the sources. It was in fact never finished, but inside it had elegant halls, beautiful high ceilings, and at its heart an octagonal chamber that may have had a revolving ceiling, allowing the diners to be showered with flower petals. The joint architects of the house were Severus and Celer, who also had a hand in much of the rest of Rome's reshaping. One popular rhyme described how the house was growing so big that it was threatening to reach the town of Veii, some ten miles distant:

> Rome's becoming a house.
> Romans, escape to Veii town,
> Unless the house
> Grows there too.

Nero himself said, "Good! Now at last I can live like a human being!" He had a statue of himself sculpted by Xenodorus, standing 120 feet high, a constant reminder to his people of what he had succeeded in achieving at their expense. This great monument was called the Colossus, and later it gave its name to the Colosseum, the

A hallway from the Golden House, one of the few structures remaining today

amphitheater built on the site during the time of the emperor Vespasian, when much of the Golden House was physically obliterated. It was buried under a mound of earth dug out to form the foundations for the new people's stadium. The Golden House itself was not rediscovered until the Renaissance period, when artists such as Michelangelo and Raphael were lowered into it on ropes so they could study the classical art found there and then model their own styles upon it. Today the Golden House is still open to visitors in Rome, a fantastic and vivid reminder of one man's megalomania.

It was the scale of the building project that made people think that Nero must have started the fire deliberately, for they reasoned that he had profited greatly from his people's grief. The ongoing Golden House project was a visible reminder of his greed and arrogance, so resentment began to build up among the plebeians, the ordinary people of Rome. Nero chose to deflect the blame for the fire and said it was the Christians who had started it. Christians were publicly executed, thrown to the beasts in the amphitheater for popular entertainment, and even burned alive, having first been doused in oil and used as torches lighting up Nero's gardens by night. In the

The so-called octagonal
room from the Golden
House

rash of persecutions that followed, Jesus's disciples, Peter and Paul, were put to death. However, this also worked against Nero, as popular opinion now came out in sympathy for the Eastern religious sect so brutally abused and tormented in this fashion. It should be made clear that this persecution was entirely political in nature. It did not spring from religious motives, as was the case in later times.

The scale of spending on the Golden House took its toll on the economy, and Nero resorted to various measures to raise money to pay for it. Six landowners in northern Africa (part of the Roman Empire) were put to death so Nero could claim their estates and the revenue from them. Measures were adopted throughout the empire to raise money, and at about this time the weight of the coinage was altered so that a gold piece, which had previously weighed one-fortieth of one pound, weighed one-forty-fifth. Nero had another plan that was seen as crazy: to connect Lake Avernus, near Naples, to the river Tiber by means of a canal, thus connecting the port of Puteoli with that of Ostia, a distance of well over 100 miles. This plan was shelved, presumably in view of the expense involved and the lack of funds available to pay for it.

A detail from paintings on the ceiling of the Golden House

THE PISONIAN CONSPIRACY

By the start of the next year, AD 65, Nero's popularity among the Roman nobility was at an all-time low. A conspiracy arose against him involving Romans from all walks of life, including senators, nobles, and plebeians. The details of the plot are very unclear. It is called the Pisonian conspiracy, after Gaius Calpurnius Piso, believed to be the leader. Piso was a man of personal charisma who was loyal to his friends and very generous. Historians believe his plan was to become emperor himself after killing Nero at games held in the Circus Maximus.

The plot was foiled because a woman named Epicharis gave information to Rear Admiral Proculus, who then notified the emperor. A series of interrogations followed, where friends and accomplices revealed each other to Nero and Tigellinus. The second guard prefect, Faenius Rufus, was an interrogator until he too was given away as a conspirator. Nineteen prominent men were killed after the plot's discovery, including the poet Lucan and Seneca, Nero's longtime adviser. The historian Tacitus remarks rather cynically that "after murdering his mother and brother, it only remained for Nero to kill his teacher and tutor." Others who lost their lives included Claudius Senecio, a close friend of Nero, and Plautius Lateranus. Piso committed suicide by cutting his veins. One of Nero's guard officers, Subrius Flavus, gave his reasons for involvement in the plot to the emperor as he was led off for execution: "I hated and detested you. I was as loyal as any soldier as long as you deserved my support. I began to hate you when you killed your father, when you murdered your mother, and destroyed your wife, when you became an actor, charioteer, and an arsonist." Nero was shocked to hear this. In the normal course of things, nobody ever dared to tell him what they thought of him face to face.

Nero rewarded the imperial guard for their loyalty by giving them 2,000 sesterces each in addition to free grain. He summoned a meeting of the Senate and awarded honorary triumphs to Publius Petronius Turpilianus, Marcus Cocceius Nerva (who would become emperor in AD 96), and Tigellinus, his guard prefect. Such triumphal honors were normally given to those who succeeded in major military campaigns, but this time Nero awarded them for saving him in the face of great danger and thus serving the state. Tigellinus's authority was extended; he

Mamertine Prison, where the Christian disciples Peter and Paul were held before they were executed. The upside-down cross in the lower right of the photo reflects a tradition that Peter was crucified upside down.

was given increased control of the guard, which became a kind of secret police force. The month of April was renamed Neroneus, in the emperor's honor.

In the same year, AD 65, Nero heard a story that Caesellius Bassus from northern Africa had seen a cave filled with the legendary Carthaginian queen Dido's treasure. With great enthusiasm, the emperor sent off a ship to gather up the collection of gold. He was enraged when he found out that the story was baseless. Later that year, Nero's wife Poppaea nagged him for returning late from the games, and in a fury he kicked her to death. She was pregnant at the time, so this was doubly hor-rific. She was given a full state funeral and her embalmed body was buried in the Mausoleum of Augustus. Some time afterward, Nero found a boy called Sporus, whom he had castrated and then married in a mock wedding ceremony because the boy reminded him of Poppaea. At another time, we are told, he also married his freedman, called Doryphorus.

After Poppaea's death, Nero took as his third wife Statilia Messallina, after putting to death her fourth husband, the consul Julius Vestinus Atticus. It seems that Nero's concept of marriage was as bizarre as many of his other ideas about life.

The second festival of the Neronia was held and Nero again performed in public, acting the parts of both men and women in a variety of roles. It is said that members of the audience often felt bored by his different performances but were compelled to sit through them. Suetonius tells us that some women pretended to give birth, while men feigned death, so they could be carried out of the shows. Others jumped off the rear wall of the theater just to escape, as the main gates were kept barred. The future emperor Vespasian was in the audience and almost fell asleep during one of Nero's performances. In view of this, Vespasian was lucky to be spared, as the emperor's enemies were by then often either killed or commanded to commit suicide for the most trivial of reasons.

Among other victims of Nero's displeasure at this time were Gaius Cassius Longinus and Lucius Junius Silanus Torquatus, the man originally betrothed to Nero's first wife Octavia. Lucius Antistius Vetus died together with his mother-in-law and daughter, as he was the father-in-law of Rubellius Plautus who had died in Asia. There were more deaths, among them Gallio and Annaeus Mela (Seneca's brothers), Rufrius Crispinus (in exile in Sardinia), and the writer Petronius, who served as the emperor's advisor on good taste. Before his death, Petronius first ensured that his collection of valuable Greek vases was smashed to pieces, as he knew Nero had desired them. Tacitus described the series of killings as "a torrent of wasted bloodshed far from the battle line of active service, which depresses the mind." Yet nothing seemed to be able to hold Nero back, and Suetonius said that no moderation prevented Nero from murdering anyone he pleased.

In AD 66, a senator of known integrity, Thrasea Paetus, was condemned to death by the Senate. It was quite clear that Nero would no longer tolerate dissension within the Senate, as Paetus had for several years withheld himself from the kind of flattery and ego massaging that the other senators had fallen into as a matter of course. His son-in-law, Helvidius Priscus, was condemned to exile at the same time.

In the same year, a great celebration was held in Rome to mark the arrival of Tiridates, the newly approved king of Armenia. Tiridates's position had been confirmed by Roman general Corbulo after a series of campaigns and diplomatic discussions on the Eastern frontier. Tiridates was the brother of Parthian king Vologeses. He had, in fact, taken the throne of Armenia by agreement with his brother, which was contrary to how the Romans normally operated. But this had been approved by Corbulo on the condition that Tiridates came in person to Rome to show his allegiance to Nero. He worshiped the emperor as his god and the gates of the Temple of Janus were closed as a sign that the Roman world was now at peace. This visit was exceptionally lavish and expensive. According to tradition, Tiridates had 3,000 followers with him from Parthia, who were looked after at huge expense for nine months, the duration of their trip to and from Rome.

There was a public coronation for the new king in the Forum and the whole city was decorated to mark the occasion. Nero set a diadem on the king's head. Nero played the kithara and drove a chariot publicly, which apparently disgusted Tiridates. However, the Eastern ruler had the sense to keep quiet about his feelings, opting instead to flatter Nero on his achievements. Privately he had much more respect for General Corbulo than for the emperor, but he kept his feelings to himself. In return, he managed to secure gifts of great value and riches needed to rebuild his capital city, Artaxata, which he also agreed to rename Neronia.

It was in September of AD 66 that Nero decided to leave Rome and embark upon a tour of Greece. Until then he had not traveled abroad, but he had often complained that his skills could only be properly understood by Greek audiences. Until then Nero's favorite place of performance in Italy had been the theater at Neapolis, or Naples, a city founded by the Greeks. He wanted to perform in the country where he felt he would be best appreciated, so he made his plans to go on tour and visit many of the main cultural centers of Greece. On his way, he collected a great number of works of art as plunder from the treasuries and temples he visited.

It is very hard for us to appreciate why Nero had a fixation with performing and how he could justify to himself what came next. Traditionally, theatrical shows and athletic events in Greece had always been put on as contests, invariably of a religious nature. Almost all of the great Greek plays were written and acted out as competition entries. The festivals at Corinth, Delphi, and Olympia had been venues for sportsmen and performers, events held at intervals of four years or so, where participants came from all around the Greek world to compete against their fellow performers. Nero decided to use his own absolute power to turn the system on its head. He left a freedman, Helius, in charge of events in Rome and took his guard prefect, Tigellinus, with him as well as the Augustans, who competed with him in the Greek games and plays. His wife, Statilia Messallina, also came as one of the party.

As Nero sailed to mainland Greece, a festival was held on Corcyra, the modern island of Corfu, and another at Actium, where the first emperor Augustus had once held games to celebrate his victory in a great battle against Mark Antony. Then Nero celebrated the so-called Isthmian Games at Corinth, where he announced the liberation of Greece. No more taxes would have to be paid to Rome, he said, and the country would have self-rule again. He then spent the winter in Greece, visiting more of the well-known centers of the arts, although it was said that he did not go to either Athens or Sparta. These two towns had been the most important centers in the country's history. Nero also did not take part in the Eleusinian Mysteries, a well-known event held near

GERMANIA

GAUL

ETRURIA

Massilia

Via Flaminia

Perus

CORSICA

Rom

N

HISPANIA

SARDINIA

SICIL

Carthage

AFRICA

Boundaries of the Roman Empire ·····················

THE ROMAN EMPIRE AT THE TIME OF NERO

BLACK SEA

ARMENIA

PONTUS

Apollonia

ASIA

PARTHIA

ACHAEA

CILICIA

SYRIA

JUDAEA

1EDITERRANEAN SEA

Alexandria

EGYPT

Berenice

Athens. The reason for this may have been an embarrassing proclamation by the master of ceremonies that called for all criminals to stay away from the celebration. Since Nero had killed his mother, he should not have been allowed to attend. In the following year, AD 67, all the main festivals were held in Greece, including a repeat of the Isthmian Games, as well as the Pythian Games at Delphi and the Olympic Games.

Nero played many parts in the Greek games and festivals, including acting in comedies and tragedies, playing the kithara, singing, and driving chariots. Even at the Olympic Games, where he fell out of his chariot and had to be helped back in again, he won first prize. In fact, everywhere he competed he was awarded the first prize, though we are told that he was always a nervous performer. It is very difficult to understand how a performer and competitor could take himself seriously knowing the outcome was so outrageously fixed, but Nero's megalomania was such that this indeed proved the case. He even contrived to hold new events at the games, such as a kithara-playing event at Olympia—which, of course, he won.

Toward the end of AD 67, Nero came to Corinth, where he held a ceremony in which he took up a golden spade and cut the first trench in the ground for a new project, a canal across the Isthmus of Corinth. He announced that this would benefit the people of Rome and himself, but conspicuously he did not mention the Senate in this, since by now he had come to disregard them in many ways. The Corinth canal would not become a finished work until many centuries later, in 1893. Nero's idea was to cut across the four-mile-wide neck of land connecting the northern part of mainland Greece to the Peloponnese, the peninsula in the south, thus making it much easier to transport goods and people around the country. Despite his best efforts, however, the project was abandoned within months of its inception.

COLLAPSE OF CONTROL

During his stay in Greece, Nero summoned before him two brothers, Rufus Sulpicius Scribonius and Proculus Sulpicius Scribonius, governors of Upper and Lower Germany. These two men had seen long service for Rome, but Nero viewed them as a threat to his position. They were required to cut their veins and commit suicide. Even worse, perhaps, the great general Cnaeus Domitius Corbulo, who had achieved so many successes for Rome along the Eastern frontier, was sentenced to death, but he actually killed himself with his dagger.

Nero may have forgotten the basis of his power, for the deaths of three such prominent generals was the signal for the army to begin questioning what was happening. It has been said that Nero managed to hold onto the support of the ordinary Romans for much of his reign and that it was the upper classes, the senators and nobles of Rome, who grew to resent his abuse of power so much. It is a fact that most army leaders were chosen from these upper classes. With the generals so shamefully removed, the upper classes began to question their ongoing acceptance of Nero and of what he was doing to Rome. Nero's reign had been a time of relative peace and calm in the empire, so there was no need for soldiers to feel under threat. Yet it was probably the very absence of military activity that indicated a lack of interest on Nero's part, and now some commanders in the army began to question their future. Their loyalty to him could be abandoned, as they saw it, because he had not been loyal to them, a prerequisite for successful empire building. They could see little chance of improvement or security until Nero was removed from office.

REVOLT

Toward the end of AD 67, the storm clouds over Nero's reign began to gather. The freedman Helius, who, much to the disgust of the Senate had been left in control of affairs in Rome, came

A detail from a mosaic depicting circus games

in person to Greece to fetch back the emperor. A famine was affecting the city because of a lack of grain ships arriving from Egypt, and there had also been an outbreak of disease in Rome. The people were already disaffected, and grew even more so when they saw cargoes of sand arriving in Rome from Alexandria to dress the arena where the imperial wrestlers would perform.

Helius was worried that the news of Nero's dalliance in Greece would make them even angrier, so he urged him to return, which the emperor did in typical style. He came first to Naples, where he celebrated his many Greek victories, and then returned to Rome, ordering a section of the city wall to be pulled down so he could enter, as was done typically for victors of the Olympic Games. He climbed to the Temple of Apollo on the Palatine Hill and dedicated 1,808 crowns that he had won in various events. The scale and the exaggeration of his successes must have repelled many of the onlookers, though it must have been an extraordinary spectacle.

By this time Nero had little or no interest at all in government. He continued to celebrate his achievements in Greece and continued to practice his performances. By March of AD 68 he was back in Naples, when news reached him

This is a bronze figurine of a soldier bearing the standard of a Roman legion.

of a revolt that had sprung up in Gallia Lugdunensis in the south of France. This was led by a Gaul named Caius Julius Vindex, whose last name meant "the avenger." Vindex had appealed to Servius Sulpicius Galba, general of Hispania Tarraconensis (Nearer Spain) for support and called for freedom from the tyrant. It seems likely that Vindex sought some kind of independence for Gaul as well as an end to Nero's rule, but Galba set his sights on becoming the next emperor. Vindex was blocked for some time by the new governor of Upper Germany, Verginius Rufus, but the revolution was under way and would prove impossible to stop. Vindex eventually committed suicide, probably in regret after seeing so many of his own people die. Verginius Rufus was urged by his soldiers to aim for the top job, but he refused to stand as a contender.

On the second of April AD 68, Galba named himself legate of the Senate and people of Rome, notably not including emperor in his title. His claim to the throne had come into the open and the challenge was there to be met. He was supported by Nero's old friend Marcus Salvius Otho, governor of Lusitania in western Spain. When Nero heard this, he fainted. Afterward, he seemed more interested in discussing the merits of a new

A carving of a Roman charioteer

water organ that had been brought to him. The reaction of the Senate, humiliated for so long by Nero, was to condemn Galba as a public enemy but also to hold discussions with him about his actions. The fact was that Galba offered them a real opportunity to emerge from the tyranny of Nero, backed as he was by the Western armies. Nero's support began to crumble and his helpers started to disappear. Tigellinus, Nero's guard prefect, simply vanished and was replaced by Nymphidius Sabinus, whose relations with the Senate were good. This was a very bad sign for Nero.

The emperor began to realize that he was beset by real problems, but failed to combat them in any meaningful way. If he had taken action by leading his armies to the west, where the rebellion had its epicenter, he may well have been able to rally considerable support from soldiers who had been loyal to his family since the time of Augustus. But as it was, his apparent cowardice took over. He asked his mistress, Calvia Crispinilla, to go to Africa to raise support, but this failed to materialize. He also summoned to Gaul the governor of Britain, Petronius Turpilianus. Nero did this to oppose the uprising, but this too had little effect, as Petronius became a supporter of Galba himself.

The historian Suetonius wrote that Nero dismissed the consuls and became sole consul himself in order to take control of events. He fell subject to deranged fantasies and thought of murdering all the senators, burning Rome, and escaping to Alexandria. When he spoke of his plans, the Senate finally acted, calling him a public enemy and stating their support for Galba, who had decided to march against Rome and take power by force. Nero suggested that if he went to Gaul and cried, standing unarmed before the battle line, the soldiers would take pity on him and relent. He considered writing songs of victory that would then be sung. The madness in him was complete, it seems, though he did decide not to make a

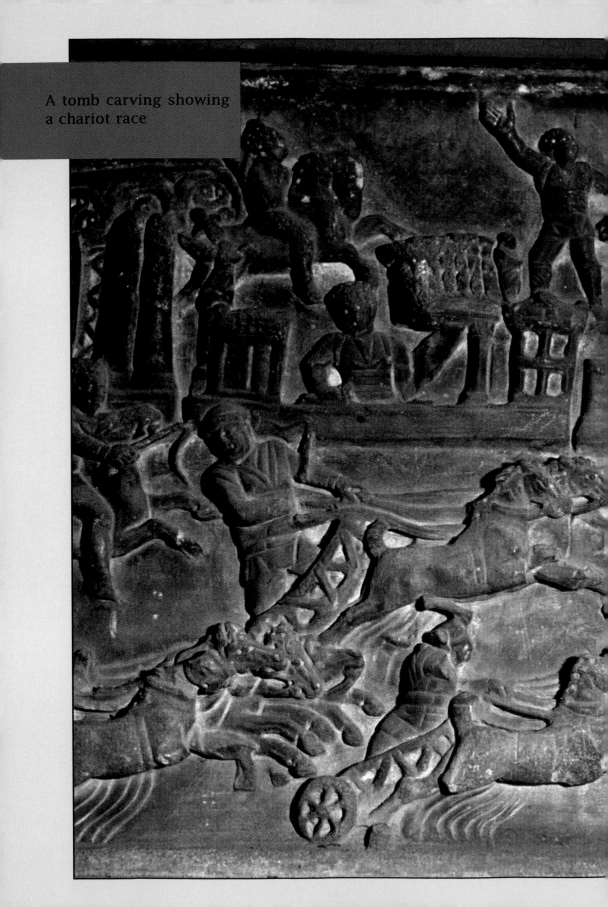

A tomb carving showing
a chariot race

speech in appeal to the people, for fear of being torn apart before reaching the Forum.

On June 8, AD 68, Nero saw that his own praetorian guards were in rebellion, too. Their new prefect, Nymphidius Sabinus, had promised to support Galba; Sabinus paid his men 30,000 sesterces each to secure their agreement. The praetorian guards now declared Nero a public enemy—the final blow to Nero's power base. Nero disguised himself in an old cloak and hat and escaped from Rome to the villa of his freedman Phaon four miles away.

Here, helped by his freedman Epaphroditus and attended by Acte, the freedwoman who had remained loyal to him throughout, Nero stabbed himself in the throat with his sword.

As he lay wounded on the floor, a centurion came in to arrest or kill him. Nero, joking even at the end of his life, said,

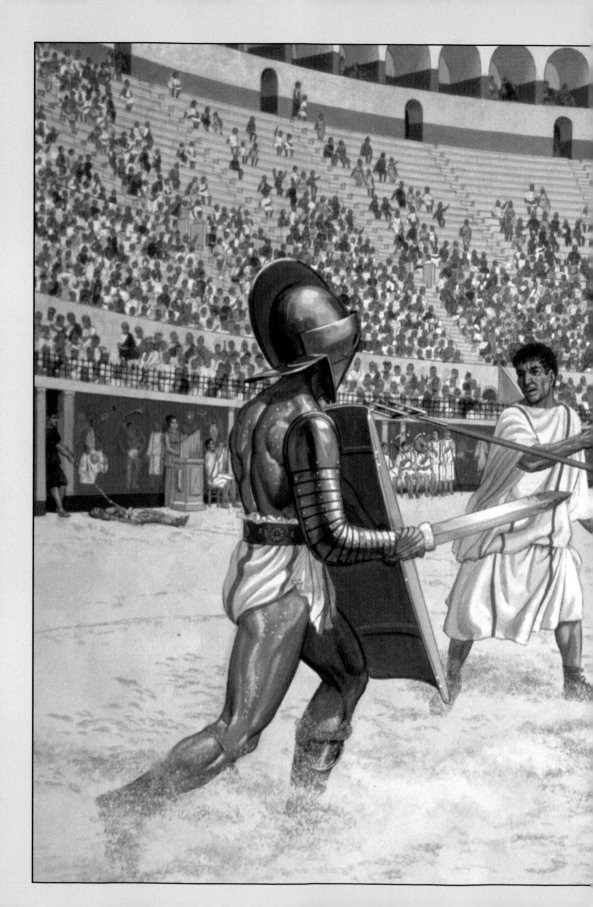

An artist's depiction of a gladiatorial combat

"What loyalty, but you are too late!" His final words were "What an artist, I die!" He was thirty years old. Acte and the nurses Ecloge and Alexandra buried his body in the family tomb of the Domitii at the Campus Martius in Rome.

Nero's legacy

Nero's life was chronicled by three Roman historians: Dio Cassius, Suetonius, and Tacitus. In each of their accounts, he is depicted as entirely evil. Of these historians, Tacitus was the only one who lived at the same time as the emperor, though at the time he was only a boy. However, the tradition that had its beginning in Tacitus's account has always been to blacken Nero's name and to see him as some kind of a monster. All three writers are guilty to some degree of sensationalism, so we must tread carefully in trying to decide exactly what may or may not be true among the many stories they told. What cannot be questioned is that Nero's reputation, his legacy to the modern world, is one tainted by the view of these authors. To get a balanced view of events, we must try to see for ourselves exactly how evil

Nero was, to what degree his name may have been disparaged unfairly, and indeed, how he was viewed in Rome after his death.

In terms of the larger empire, Nero had shown limited interest in government; little had been done during his reign to expand or consolidate Roman rule abroad.

There had been major unrest in Britain in AD 60, when the revolt of Boudicca had wiped out around 70,000 inhabitants of Colchester, London, and St. Albans. Boudicca was queen of a tribe called the Iceni. When her husband Prasutagus died, the Romans refused to acknowledge her authority. Boudicca's daughters were raped and she was assaulted, precipitating her terrible revenge. Her revolt threatened to cause the Romans to abandon the province of Britain entirely. However, Governor Suetonius Paulinus put down the rebellion. Boudicca died, and stability in the province was restored. At this stage, the drive was to extend Roman control northward, beyond the legionary bases at Exeter, Lincoln, and the many other encampments that were spread out around the province. Plans to do this matured gradually, and within the next twenty years or so, three major new bases for the legions were built at Caerleon, Chester, and York. It should be observed, though, that this was not so much Nero's own policy as the continuation of what Claudius had first started in AD 43.

On the Eastern frontier, problems with the Parthians had been ongoing for many years, but especially since AD 55, when rival challenges for the Armenian throne arose in the north. This was very much at the edge of the Roman world and the Parthians were an unpredictable force. Their king, Vologeses, had appointed his brother Tiridates as the king of Armenia, as previously described. But Nero had refused to accept this and later appointed another man, Tigranes, in his place. Various cities were captured and then recaptured, including Volandum and Artaxata, which were destroyed by Romans under the command of Corbulo. Nero was hailed as imperator and a triumph was held in Rome in AD 58 to celebrate a great victory. However, this was a hollow claim, and the problems in Armenia were far from solved.

Eventually war broke out between Tigranes and Tiridates, while the Romans sided first with one and then the other. There was even disagreement between Corbulo and Lucius Caesennius Paetus, governor of Syria who had

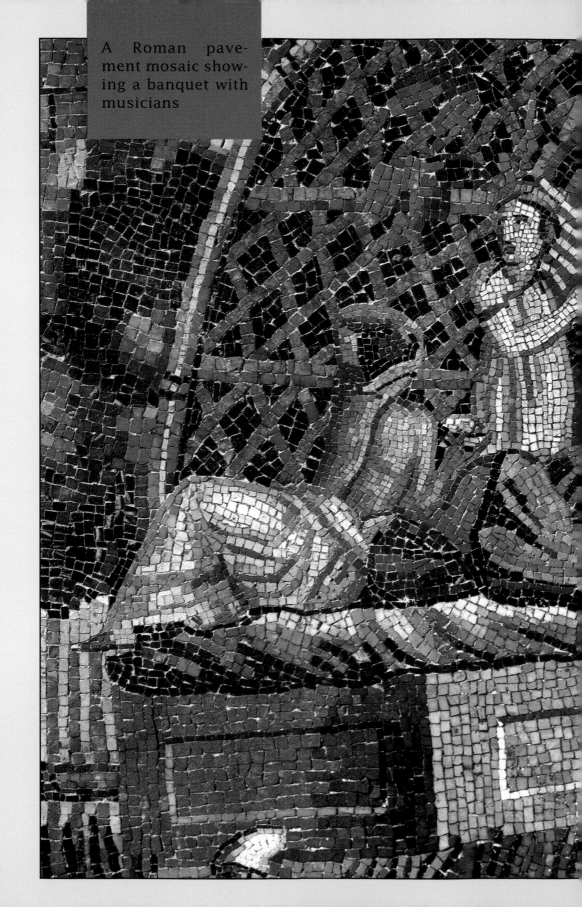

A Roman pavement mosaic showing a banquet with musicians

been sent by Nero to help. This resulted in Paetus being defeated by Tiridates and his men, while Corbulo came in afterward to pick up the pieces. The eventual outcome was that Tiridates publicly took off his crown and laid it before a statue of Nero in the field, agreeing to come to Rome and receive it back from the emperor in person. The history of the Armenian campaign is a very messy one and won the emperor little glory, though he was again acclaimed as imperator on the arrival of Tiridates in Rome.

The only other area of major conflict under Nero's reign was in Judea, modern-day Israel, where rebellion had broken out in AD 66 and was dealt with by the very capable future emperor Vespasian. This was an extremely serious situation that led in turn to the sack of Jerusalem in AD 70 by Titus, Vespasian's son, and to the dismantling of the Hebrew kingdom. Toward the end of his reign, the situation was threatening and unclear as the Roman forces attempted to deal with the situation.

One thing that certainly comes across in all accounts is Nero's tremendous enthusiasm, though it was so often misguided. His all-consuming passion for the theater and performance sets him apart from all other emperors and members of his social class, and it is referred to repeatedly by historians of the Roman period. Dio Cassius mentions a speech made by Julius Vindex during the revolt in Gaul, where he says that Nero disgraced the names of Caesar and Augustus through his acting and passion for theater. In order to understand how repellent this was at the time, one must understand that Nero used his position as emperor to secure a place on the stage and compel an audience of the Roman nobility to offer their applause. Secondly, during that time, being an actor was not regarded as a fit occupation for an emperor or any upper-class Roman citizen. In this, Nero's self-degradation was obvious to all who witnessed his antics.

Nero's great love for participation in sport led him to coerce many of his countrymen, the Augustans in particular, to take part in games such as the Neronia in AD 60 and AD 65. Suetonius writes that Nero compelled 400 senators and 600 nobles to do battle in the amphitheater. It is hard to imagine that these people all participated willingly, even if the numbers have been exaggerated. During Nero's trip to Greece, he took a large number of followers with him, including the Augustans, whose job must have been to compete in events against

A wall carving of a Roman money bag, with an inscription that reads "A Traveler to the Treasury"

Nero. The sheer number of prizes he won—1,808 in total—shows how much their role was merely a token, or a support mechanism for massaging one man's ego. Effectively, their job was to lose or be runners-up to their boss. In this, we see how misguided his enthusiasm to perform was, as it led him to humiliate so many of those who should have been his genuine supporters.

The historians also state that the promotion of freedmen to senior positions led to discontent, such as when Anicetus was put in charge of the fleet at Misenum and Helius was left in charge of affairs in Rome during the emperor's time in Greece. Helius was accused of abusing his position by Dio Cassius as he was apparently guilty of putting to death Sulpicius Camerinus, a leading senator. This must have been hard to accept for those who saw the freedman as a social inferior brought to prominence on the whim of the emperor. Nero's predecessor, Claudius, had also been accused many times of giving away excessive authority to his private staff of freedmen, and this brought him into disrepute with many of the senators. Nero had sworn on his accession not to fall into the same habits, but it became clear that he made this promise without any sincerity.

Other promises made at the beginning of Nero's rule included one that he would not, as Claudius had done so often, hold trials behind closed doors. But toward the end of his reign, it appears that Nero's system of justice was entirely arbitrary. So many deaths are mentioned in all the sources that we cannot assume them all to be lies. Nero clearly removed anyone he perceived to stand in his way without compunction or real reason. Tacitus says that Pallas, the ex-freedman of Claudius, was killed for being too rich, and Suetonius says that Thrasea Paetus's flaw was looking like a grumpy old schoolmaster. In fact, Nero was always jealous of anyone else who caught public attention. This seems to have been a crime that only the bold around him would dare commit. In the same way, when the emperor did confer liberty to his subjects, it was seen as a gift conferred by an all-powerful ruler, not a right. By these tokens, we can see that the resentment building up against Nero was quite real and justified.

Nero's private life has been variously described by historians, but all seem to agree that he had multiple marriages to women and to men, some of whom seem to have been chosen deliberately for their strange habits. He seems to have publicly acted out his sexual perversions, and Suetonius mentions that he forced the wives of Roman noblemen to act as prostitutes in temporary brothels, serving not only his own needs but those of anyone else. This took place during a barge trip from Rome to Ostia and, if true, can only have aggravated the bad feelings growing toward Nero among the senators and nobles. Even if exaggerated, this story shows how

The virgin goddess Vesta, seated, with four vestal virgins

Nero was viewed shortly after his death. If the story had not been believable, it would probably not have been included. Another story passed on by Suetonius says that Nero raped a vestal virgin called Rubria. This is not mentioned by the other two writers and could well be untrue, like many accounts in modern-day tabloid newspapers. However, if we consider that the modern-day equivalent of a vestal virgin would be a nun, the act described would have been truly horrific.

Suetonius refers to Nero's dreadful treatment of the Senate, mentioning how he sometimes seized the estates of those who had died but had not left enough of their possessions to him as emperor. Suetonius also claims that when appointing magistrates, Nero said, "You know what I need. Let's see that nobody else is left with anything." The constant plundering of property was needed to pay for all the excesses that went with Nero's reign, and for the first time since Augustus became emperor, money was always in short supply. Again, the impact of this must have been considerable, as upper-class Romans saw the state coffers become depleted through one man's lust and greed.

One of the most horrific crimes committed by Nero was that of matricide, the murder of his mother, Agrippina. In an ordinary Roman's eyes, family unity was very important, and a man's mother was to be honored.

The repeated mention of incest between the emperor and his mother is a reminder of how degraded the relationship was considered to be at the time, and the calculated plotting of her death shows Nero in

A bust of a Roman noblewoman wearing an elaborate wig

a terrible light. Tacitus mentions that at Nero's birth, a fortuneteller had predicted that he would kill his mother and become emperor, but Agrippina had said, "Let him kill me, provided that he becomes emperor." There seems to be little doubt that he actually did kill her and little doubt that he enjoyed doing so.

Nero's crimes included a program of persecutions against the Christians, which started sometime after the great fire in AD 64. Nero may have had his reasons for setting this train of events into motion, but his excessive cruelty must have offended many who witnessed it, Christian and non-Christian. The new faith had recently spread from the province of Judea (modern-day Israel) and was beginning to make an impact on Rome itself, where several of its guiding principles clashed strongly with the accepted state religion. The group of established Roman gods was headed by Jupiter Optimus Maximus, or Jupiter the Greatest and Best, whose control of divine forces was mirrored in human terms by the emperor's control of his people. Christianity threatened this system. Its followers maintained that since there was only one god, Jupiter and his fellow gods did not exist. This belief was supported by the beliefs of another non-Christian sect from Judea that the Romans sometimes confused with the Christians. These were the Jews, who believed that there was only one god and that they were his chosen people. While the normally adaptable Romans would accept new gods into their system and remain perfectly happy about it, these two new religious groups from Judea both had faiths that made it impossible for Romans to accept them. Nero was in some sense really reacting against a religion that threatened the very fabric of Roman society. His persecution of Christians has to be seen in this light to be fully understood, though it certainly does not justify his reaction. Nero's reputation with future generations was greatly colored by this affair. The European tradition that has blackened his name and portrayed him as an evil

A Roman coin with a profile of Nero

monster is a Christian tradition. It is perhaps his assault on the Christians and his responsibility for the deaths of Peter and Paul, in particular, that have caused him to remain a hated figure throughout history.

Strange though it seems, however, Nero is often written about by historians as a whimsical figure. His sense of humor combined with his passion for all kinds of performance endears him to the reader and gives him a kind of charm, though this may be hard to accept given his brutality and horrendous behavior. One cannot help but see him as a larger-than-life, misguided bundle of energy and enthusiasm, who even made jokes at his own death. We can see him falling off his chariot at Olympia and still not really caring, safe in the knowledge that he would win the race anyway. When Lucius Caesennius Paetus returned to Rome from his failed campaign in Armenia, he is said to have been terrified of what Nero might do to him. But Nero actually let him off, saying that he thought it was unfair to keep such a timid man in suspense as to what might happen to him. Nero was bound to be rejected by the senators and nobles whom he had for so long humiliated. Yet none of this lessens our interest in hearing more about him or our fascination with all the other things he might have said or done.

After Nero's death, the Roman world experienced major political turmoil and was turned on its head for at least twelve months while four men vied for supreme control. Each of the four men—Galba, Otho, Vitellius, and Vespasian—became, in turn, the emperor of Rome, supported and brought to power by their own military factions. Nero's legacy (as the last of the Julian line) was to see the transfer of power change from being a dynastic, family-driven process to a competitive system where the most powerful army general would have the best chance of success. It is true that once Vespasian took over a new dynasty was begun, that of the Flavians, and that gradually stability returned to Rome. It seemed for a while that the old days were back when the empire could be inherited, but in reality this proved short-lived.

There were many left after his death who did mourn Nero genuinely, however. In looking at portraits of the emperor, it is possible to see him like we see rock stars today, an Elvis Presley figure perhaps, with a curling lip and a strangely captivating smile who after his death was regularly "seen" by people all over the world. Nero imitators who sang to the accompaniment of the kithara turned up in different parts of the empire, as if the Romans could not accept that their larger-than-life emperor had actually died. His mythology lived on for many years after his death, finding its way into literature and popular folklore alike. Such is the legacy of Nero, whose story will always be available to fascinate us.

WHAT HAPPENED AFTERWARD?

Immediately after the death of Nero, Servius Sulpicius Galba became the next emperor of Rome, until his death in early AD 69. He did not realize that the extent of his power was due to the praetorian guards. He failed to pay them properly, so they turned against him and killed him.

Marcus Salvius Otho became emperor of Rome after causing a rebellion and deposing Galba. He was defeated by the forces of Vitellius and committed suicide in April of AD 69. Tigellinus disappeared as guard prefect in early AD 68 and was officially replaced by a colleague, Nymphidius Sabinus. Sabinus was forced to commit suicide during the rule of Otho in early AD 69. Tiridates was removed from power as king of Armenia in AD 72, when a tribe called the Alans marched against his kingdom. He was not mentioned again in historical sources.

Titus Flavius Vespasianus (Vespasian) raised a rival claim to the throne against Vitellius in July AD 69. He caused Vitellius's downfall and established a new dynasty, the Flavians, as rulers of Rome. After his death in AD 79, his sons Titus and Domitian became the next emperors.

HOW DO WE KNOW?

Primary sources for Nero fall into two types. The first type is written evidence from three ancient accounts: Dio Cassius in books 61 to 63 of his *Roman History*, Tacitus in the *Annals of Imperial Rome*, and imperial biographer Suetonius. Secondly, there is also a wealth of archaeological evidence found in the city of Rome itself, including the Golden House that Nero built, as well as in other outposts of the empire. Also important are inscriptions on public buildings throughout the empire, as well as coinage, which provides valuable portraiture and other information.

Glossary

colonia A Roman town or settlement where all the inhabitants had the status of full Roman citizens.

consul The title given to a very senior Roman magistrate, a man who had reached the top of the *cursus honorum*. There were always two consuls chosen at any one time, in theory so one could overrule the other. It is the equivalent in modern-day terms to a prime minister or president, though in imperial times a consul was still subject to the emperor. However, under the emperors it was seen as desirable for as many senior Romans as possible to reach the top job, so there was usually more than one set of consuls chosen in one year. The emperor sometimes served as consul himself.

consul designate Someone who was selected for the job of consul in an upcoming year.

Forum Romanum The Forum was the center of Rome. It consisted of many public buildings, including temples, shops, and law courts.

freedman A person who once had been a slave but was later released. Freedmen often continued to maintain a social and business relationship with their ex-masters and, in particular, freedmen were often employed as trusted individuals by the emperors.

imperator This title was given to a general who had been victorious in battle. It was often used as a term to indicate the emperor himself, but had its origins in military life.

kithara An instrument similar to a guitar (the word "guitar" in fact derives from kithara), having strings and played to accompany someone singing. It is also often referred to as a lyre or a harp.

plebeian This term was given to a member of the plebs, the ordinary people of Rome. It is used to distinguish lower-class citizens from the rest of society.

republic This term is often used for the Roman state, represented by the acronym SPQR, meaning the Senate and People of Rome. After Augustus became the first emperor of Rome, the republic was, in effect, an empire controlled by one man, but the illusion was maintained carefully that the republic still existed and that the Senate and people were as important as they had always been in Rome's early history.

Senate A body of about 600 senior statesmen whose authority combined with the emperor's. The Senate acted as the lawgiving body of Rome; its importance in Roman history cannot be overestimated.

toga   A woolen garment worn by Romans. A ceremony took place when a boy put on a man's toga for the first time, usually around the age of fourteen. It was a big event in a young person's life.

FOR MORE INFORMATION

ORGANIZATIONS

The American Classical League
(National Junior Classical League)
Miami University
Oxford, OH 45056
(513) 529-7741
e-mail: info@aclclassics.org
Web site: http://www.aclclassics.org

American Philological Association
University of Pennsylvania
292 Logan Hall
249 South 36th Street
Philadelphia, PA 19104-6304
(215) 898-4975
e-mail: apaclassics@sas.upenn.edu
Web site: http://www.apaclassics.org

Classical Association of New England
Department of Classical Studies
Wellesley College
106 Central Street
Wellesley, MA 02481
e-mail: rstarr@wellesley.edu
Web site: http://www.wellesley.edu/
   ClassicalStudies/cane/index.html

WEB SITES

Due to the changing nature of Internet links, the Rosen Publishing Group, Inc., has developed an online list of Web sites related to the subject of this book. This site is updated regularly. Please use this link to access the list:

http://www.rosenlinks.com/lar/nero/

FOR FURTHER READING

Baker, Rosalie, and Charles Baker. *Ancient Romans*. Oxford, England: Oxford University Press, 1998.

Connolly, Peter, and Hazel Dodge. *The Ancient City: Life in Classical Athens and Rome*. Oxford, England: Oxford University Press, 1998.

Cornell, Tim, and John Matthews. *Atlas of the Roman World*. Oxford, England: Phaidon, 1982.

Petren, Birgitta, and Elizabetta Putini. *Why Are You Calling Me a Barbarian?* Los Angeles: Getty Trust, 1999.

Salway, Peter. *The Oxford Illustrated History of Roman Britain*. Oxford, England: Oxford University Press, 1993.

BIBLIOGRAPHY

PRIMARY SOURCES

Dio Cassius. *Roman History, Books 61 to 70*. Cambridge, England: Loeb Classical Library, 2000.

Suetonius. *The Twelve Caesars.* London: Penguin, 1957.

Tacitus. *The Annals of Imperial Rome.* London: Penguin, 1956.

SECONDARY SOURCES

Bishop, John. *Nero: The Man and the Legend.* New York: A. S. Barnes, 1965.

Claridge, Amanda. *Rome.* Oxford, England: Oxford University Press, 1998.

Cook, S. A., et al. *The Cambridge Ancient History, Volume X.* Cambridge, England: Cambridge University Press, 1966.

Franzero, Charles Marie. *The Life and Times of Nero.* London: A. Redman, 1954.

Grant, Michael. *Nero.* London: Weidenfeld & Nicolson, 1970.

Griffin, Miriam T. *Nero: The End of a Dynasty*.
London: Batsford, 1984.

Scullard, Hugh H. *From the Gracchi to Nero*. London:
Methuen, 1959.

INDEX

ABOUT THE AUTHOR

Julian Morgan earned his B.A. in Greek studies at Bristol University, England, in 1979. He also earned a master's degree in computers and education at King's College, London, in 1990. He is currently head of classics at Derby Grammar School. Julian has a special interest in software design and has published many programs, including ROMANA and Rome the Eternal City, through his business, J-PROGS. He is a member of the American Classical League's Committee on Educational Computer Applications. He is the computing coordinator for the Joint Association of Classical Teaching (JACT) and has a regular column, "Computanda," in their bulletin. He also runs a training business called Medusa, which specializes in helping teachers of classics to use information technology in their teaching.

CREDITS

EDITOR
Jake Goldberg

LAYOUT
Geri Giordano

SERIES DESIGN
Evelyn Horovicz